Quotes for Personal Excellence – 9

Leadership & Teamwork

One Hundred Quotes and Thoughts
with One Hundred Insightful Illustrations of Lord Ganesha

R.N. Kogata • Lalita Kogata

DK PRINTWORLD
Publishers of Indian Traditions

First Published in India, 2015
ISBN 13: 978-81-246-0761-9
ISBN 10: 81-246-0761-3

A creation of:
Mr R.N. Kogata and Mrs Lalita Kogata
608, Hiran Magari, Sector - 11, Udaipur, India
Phones: +91-94141 58870, +91-294-258 3870
devkush@rediffmail.com

Printed and published by:
D.K. Printworld (P) Ltd.
'Vedasri', F-395, Sudarshan Park
(Metro Station: Ramesh Nagar), New Delhi - 110 015
Phones: 011-2545 3975 / 2546 6019   Fax: 011-2546 5926
e-mail: indology@dkprintworld.com   Web: www.dkprintworld.com

Preface

Leadership is a word and a concept that has been more argued than almost any other. One should not be one of the desk-pounding types that like to stick out his jaw and look like he is bossing the show. One should far rather get behind and, recognizing the frailties and the requirements of human nature, should rather try to persuade a man to go along, because once you have persuaded him, he will stick. If you scare him, he will stay just as long as he is scared, and then he is gone.

You cannot do all the work that is expected from you and hence, there is a need of a team. Fostering teamwork is creating a work culture that values collaboration. In a teamwork environment, people understand and believe that thinking, planning, decisions and actions are better when done cooperatively. People recognize, and even assimilate, the belief that "none of us is as good as all of us". However, it's hard to find work places that exemplify teamwork. Teamwork generates conflicts. People have different ideas and they wish to do things differently. Ambiguity in purpose, and undefined roles and objectives also proves to be hurdle in success.

Normally most of us are very bad players of teamwork. Each member of the team wants to hog the limelight, wants to take the credit for the "success" of the team and "love to blame" his team-member for the failure of his team. Be it any team; small or big, we normally failed as a team. Hard to digest, but this is a fact. Some of the factors our failures as a team are ego, arrogance, lack of knowledge, confidence and self belief, insecurity, and due to this, we tend to block others' success. We tend to harm them. We tend to play "political games" with your own team-members. You can, however, create a teamwork culture by doing just a few things right.

There is a saying in Hindi, "Yatha Raja, Tatha Praja" (as the king, so the people). Hence, the team leader has an important role in "team development and management". Just because you work in teams or lead teams doesn't mean that you are a good team player. A team leader should have confidence in his own abilities, knowledge and skills.

In life, it doesn't matter where you're coming from, where are you going and how are you going to get there? Aside from what you want to accomplish, what kind of a person do you want to become as the result of all your work and effort? Men and women who achieve great things in life are invariably those who give a lot of thought to their own evolution and growth. They become exceptional people by design, not by accident. They are like master craftsmen, continually shaping and polishing their characters and personalities so that they evolve and grow into someone important and worthwhile. And so should you. The highest goal you can have for yourself is to become a leader, to become an outstanding man or woman who is looked up to, admired and respected by the people around you.

We have been led to believe, over the years, that leaders are those who stride boldly, exude power and confidence, give orders and make decisions for others to carry out. However, that's an old school of thought. The leader of today is the one who asks questions, listens carefully, plans diligently and then builds consensus among all the stakeholders for achieving the goals. A leader does not try to do it by himself or herself. A leader is a person who gets things done by helping others to help themselves. The mark of true leaders is that they lead the action. They are willing to go first. They set the example and act as the role model. They do what they expect others to do. A key leadership characteristic is to set high standards of accountability for themselves and for their behaviours. They assume that others are watching them and then setting their own standards by what they do.

Always strive to lengthen your stride. If you stride so that you are comfortable, you will never improve. You must stretch yourself. The secret to accomplishing much is to reach beyond your grasp! If your reach exceeds your grasp, you will enter a daily fight of self-discipline and self-denial. Start every day with the intention, determination and commitment to do what others are unwilling to do.

To be a successful leader, one should be willing to grow, work harder and smarter than anyone else, always be grateful, always be selfless, never be satisfied, love everyone and everything, live right now, give best at all times, think on spirit not on matter, believe in God, always look inward and upward and not outward, believe in the power of an idea, trust and know that all is well, and never give up and live the Dream.

To understand the leadership and teamwork in a simple way, we have conceived the idea of this book to tell you much more on leadership an teamwork in just few hours.

Preface

These meaningful quotes about leadership and teamwork will touch, inspire and move you, and you can thus have a line of action and thoughts to be a Great Leader.

This book provides 100 carefully chosen quotations on Leadership & Teamwork, mixed, modified and created. Some of the thoughts presented are ours and others are from the people who have stood by and worked for the values; some were famous names and some others were ordinary people. We have tried to indicate in the acknowledgement page name of the persons who have quoted wherever we could remember. Our sincere thanks to all these great personalities and eminent writers; who have given such invaluable thoughts to this world. Any amendment/addition in this regard is most welcome from the readers.

Ganesha gives peace, prosperity and wisdom also and, therefore, each of the quotes in this book has a painting of Lord Ganesha to inspire you. These paintings have been created by our professional artists keeping in view the theme of individual quote.

We prostrate before our parents Smt Kanchan Devi and Shri Bhairav Lal Kogata, and late Kamla Devi Nuwal and late Prof. K.M. Nuwal, whose blessings have enabled us to grow in life.

With the expectation of blessings and constructive feedback from all of you.

Lalita & R.N. Kogata

Leadership & Teamwork

One Hundred Quotes and Thoughts
with One Hundred Insightful Illustrations of Lord Ganesha

Acknowledgement

Quotations from some eminent writers, philosophers and great personalities have been included in this book. Details of the same are given below. We sincerely thank all of them.

Page No.	Quotation by	Page No.	Quotation by	Page No.	Quotation by	Page No.	Quotation by
L-1	Russell H. Ewing	L-27	Jack Welch	L-51	Lewis H. Lapham	L-78	Walter Lippmann
L-2	Franklin Roosevelt	L-28	Warren G. Bennis	L-53	Jesse Jackson	L-79	Max De Pree
L-4	John C. Maxwell	L-29	J.D. Rockefeller	L-54	Grace Hopper	L-80	Jim Rohn
L-6	John C. Maxwell	L-30	Colin Powell	L-55	John G. Agno	L-81	Kenneth Blanchard
L-7	Ralph Nader	L-32	Mac Anderson	L-56	John C. Maxwell	L-82	Eric Hoffer
L-8	John C. Maxwell	L-33	Pat Riley	L-57	Lance Secretan	L-83	Clarence Randall
L-9	George W. Bush	L-34	Don Shula	L-58	Dwight D. Eisenhower	L-85	Peter F. Drucker
L-10	Jack Welch	L-35	Lao-Tzu	L-60	Bill Bradley	L-86	Brian Koval
L-11	David R. Gergen	L-36	Mahatma Gandhi	L-61	Jim Rohn	L-87	Margaret Carty
L-12	James Allen	L-37	Indira Gandhi	L-62	John Heywood	L-88	Henry Kissinger
L-13	Sam J. Ervin, Jr.	L-38	Henry Ford	L-63	Booker T. Washington	L-89	James Buchanan
L-14	Daisaku Ikeda	L-39	John Quincy Adams	L-64	Dennis A. Peer	L-90	Martin Luther King, Jr.
L-16	Vanna Bonta	L-40	Ken Blanchard	L-65	Arnold H. Glasow	L-91	Edith Wharton
L-17	Patrick Lencioni	L-41	Vince Lombardi	L-66	Master Jin Kwon	L-92	Joe Namath
L-18	Bill Gates	L-42	Ryunosuke Satoro	L-67	Ken Blanchard	L-93	Harry Truman
L-19	Jack Welch	L-43	Steve Jobs	L-68	John C. Maxwell	L-95	John C. Maxwell
L-20	Vince Lombardi	L-44	Nelson Mandela	L-69	Bill Bradley	L-96	Philip Crosby
L-21	John C. Maxwell	L-45	Lloyd Dobens	L-70	Reed Markham	L-98	Joe Paterno
L-22	John C. Maxwell	L-46	Joe Klock	L-72	J. Michael Straczynski	L-99	Friedensreich H.
L-23	Dee Hock	L-47	Ross Perot	L-73	John C. Maxwell	L-100	Theodore H. White
L-24	Ralph W. Emerson	L-48	Warren G. Bennis	L-75	Jim Loehr		
L-25	John Kotter	L-49	Mike Murdock	L-76	Theodore Roosevelt		
L-26	Casey Stengel	L-50	Mark A. Clement	L-77	Jim Rohn		

A boss creates fear,
a leader confidence.

A boss fixes blame,
a leader corrects mistakes.

A boss knows all,
a leader asks questions.

A boss makes work drudgery,
a leader makes it interesting.

A boss is interested in himself;
a leader is interested in the group.

L-1

A good leader cannot get too far ahead of his followers.

A good leader inspires people
to have confidence in him;

a great leader inspires people
to have confidence in themselves.

A good leader is a person
who takes a little more
than his share of the blame
and a little less
than his share of the credit.

A great leader
attracts great people
and knows
how to hold them together.

L-5

A great leader's courage
to fulfil his vision
comes from passion,
not by position.

A leader has the vision
and conviction that
a dream can be achieved.

He inspires
the power and energy
to get it done.

A leader is one
who knows the way,
goes the way,
and shows the way.

A leader is someone, who

I. Under-promises and over-delivers.

ii. Can do everything himself,
but allows other people help him.

iii. Brings people together.

iv. Mobilizes others
toward a goal shared by
leaders and followers.

v. Is acknowledged as such.

A leader's job is
to look into the future
and see the organization,
not as it is,
but as it should be.

L-10

A leader's role is
to raise people's aspirations
for what they can become
and
to release their energies
so that they will try to get there.

A man has to learn
that he can't command things,
but that he can command himself;

that he can't coerce the wills of others,
but that he can mould
and master his own will;

things serve him who serves Truth;

and people seek guidance of him
who is master of himself.

A person,
who is worthy of being a leader,
wants power not for himself,
but in order to be of service.

A person who,
no matter how
desperate the situation,
gives others hope,
is a true leader.

A real leader faces the music,
even when
he does not like the tune.

Any leader
who doesn't support
the heart of evolving humanity
is not a leader
worthy of being followed.

As a leader,
you're probably not doing a good job
unless your employees can do
a good impression of you
when you're not around.

As we look ahead
into the future,
leaders will be those
who empower others.

Before you are a leader,
success is all about growing yourself.
When you become a leader,
success is all about growing others.

Build for your team
a feeling of oneness,
of dependence on one another
and of strength
to be derived by unity.

Character creates consistency,
and if your people know
what they can expect from you,
they will continue to look to you
for leadership.

L-21

Character makes
trust possible,
and
trust is the foundation
of leadership.

L-22

Control is not leadership;
management is not leadership;
leadership is leadership.

If you seek to lead,
invest at least 50% of your time
in leading yourself —
your own purpose, ethics,
principles, motivation, and conduct.

Invest at least 20% leading those
with authority over you

and invest 30% leading your peers.

Do not follow where
the path may lead.

Go instead where
there is no path
and leave a trail.

Effective leaders help others
to understand the necessity of change
and to accept a common vision
of the desired outcome.

Finding good players is easy.

Getting them to play
as a team
is another story.

Good business leaders
create a vision,
articulate the vision,
passionately own the vision,
and
relentlessly drive it to completion.

Good leaders
make people feel that
they're at the very heart of things,
not at the periphery.

Good leadership consists of showing average people how to do the work of superior people.

Great leaders are
almost always great simplifiers,
who can cut through argument, debate,
and doubt to offer a solution
everybody can understand.

Great leaders are rare,
so I am following myself.

Great leadership
usually starts with
a willing heart,
a positive attitude,
and
a desire to make
a difference.

Great teamwork
is the only way we create
the breakthroughs that
define our careers.

I do not know any other way to lead,
but by example.

I have three precious things
which I hold fast and prize.

The first is gentleness;
the second is frugality;
the third is humility, which keeps me
from putting myself before others.

Be gentle and you can be bold;
be frugal and you can be liberal;
avoid putting yourself before others
and you can become a leader
among men.

I offer you peace.

I offer you love.

I offer you friendship.

I see your beauty.

I hear your need.

I feel your feelings.

My wisdom flows
from the Highest Source.

I salute that Source in you.

Let us work together
for unity and love.

I suppose
leadership at one time
meant muscle power;

but today it means
getting along with people.

If everyone
moves forward together,
then success
takes care of itself.

If your actions inspire others
to dream more, learn more,
do more and become more,
you are a leader.

In the past a leader was a boss.

Today's leaders must be partners with their people . . . they no longer can lead solely based on positional power.

Individual commitment
to a group effort
makes a teamwork,
a company work,
a society work,
a civilization work.

L-41

Individually, we are one drop.

Together, we are an ocean.

Innovation distinguishes
between
a leader and a follower.

L-43

It is better to lead from behind
and to put others in front,
when you celebrate victory
or nice things occur.

You take the front line
when there is danger.

People will appreciate
your leadership.

It is not a question of
how well each process works;

the question is
how well they all work together.

It is the very essence of good leadership
to give away all credit
for positive achievement,
to identify only team goals, and
always refer to them as such.

Lead and inspire people.
Don't try to manage
and manipulate them.

Inventories can be managed
but people must be led.

Leaders do not avoid,
repress, or deny conflict,
but rather see it
as an opportunity.

L-48

Leaders
make decisions
that create
the future
they desire.

Leaders who win the respect of others
are the ones who deliver
more than they promise,

not the ones who promise
more than they can deliver.

Leadership consists
not in degrees of technique
but in traits of character;
it requires moral rather than
athletic or intellectual effort,
and it imposes on both
the leader and follower alike
the burdens of self-restraint.

Leadership deals with
what are the things
to be accomplished.

Management deals with
how those things
can be best accomplished.

Leadership has a harder job to do than just choose sides.

It must bring sides together.

Leadership is a two-way street,
loyalty up and loyalty down.

Respect for one's superiors;
care for one's crew.

Leadership is applicable to all facets of life:
a competency that you can learn
to expand your perspective,
set the context of a goal,
understand the dynamics of
human behaviour and
take the initiative to get to
where you want to be.

Leadership is getting people
to help you when they
are not obligated to do so.

Leadership is not so much
about technique and methods
as it is about opening the heart.

It is about inspiration
of oneself and of others.

Great leadership is about
human experiences, not processes.

Leadership is not a formula or a program,
it is a human activity that comes
from the heart and considers
the hearts of others.

It is an attitude, not a routine.

L-57

Leadership is
the art of getting
someone else to do
something you want to do,
because he wants to do it.

Leadership is the wise use of power.

Power is the capacity
to translate vision and intention
into reality and sustain it.

Leadership unlocks
people's potential
to become better.

Managers help people see themselves as they are.

Leaders help people to see themselves better than what they are.

Many hands
make work light.

Most leaders spend time trying
to get others think highly of them.

Instead, they should try
to get their people think
more highly of themselves.

It's wonderful when the people
believe in their leader.

It's more wonderful when
the leader believes in his people!

You can't hold a man down
without staying down with him.

One measure of leadership is
the calibre of people who
choose to follow you.

One of the true tests
of leadership is the ability to recognize
and address a problem
before it becomes an emergency.

One piece of log
creates a small fire,
adequate enough
to warm you up.

Add a few more pieces of log
to blast an immense bonfire,
large enough to warm up
your entire circle of friends;

needless to say that
individuality counts
but teamwork dynamites.

People do not care
how much you know
until they know
how much you care.

People do not mind
being challenged to do better
if they know that the request
is coming from a caring heart.

Respect your fellow human being,
treat them fairly,
disagree with them honestly,
enjoy their friendship,
explore your thoughts about
one another candidly,
work together for a common goal
and help one another
to achieve it.

Successful leaders see opportunities
in every difficulty
rather than
difficulty in every opportunity.

T — Together

E — Everyone

A — Achieve

M— More

That is Team.

Take care, do not fight, and remember:

if you don't choose to lead,
you will forever be led by others.

Find what scares you, and do it.

You can make a difference,
if you choose to do so.

Teams
make you better than you are,
multiply your value,
enable you to do what you do best,
allow you to help others do their best,
give you more time,
provide you with companionship,
help you fulfil the desires of your heart
and compound your vision and effort.

Teamwork is the ability
to work together
toward a common vision.

It's the ability
to direct individual accomplishments
toward organizational objectives.

It is the fuel
that allows common people
to attain uncommon results.

The ability to summon positive emotions
during periods of intense stress
lies at the heart of effective leadership.

The best leader is the one
who has sense enough to pick up
good men to do
what he wants to do,
and self-restraint to keep away
from meddling with them
while they do it.

L-76

The challenge of leadership
is to be strong, but not rude;

be kind, but not weak;

be bold, but not bully;

be thoughtful, but not lazy;

be humble, but not timid;

be proud, but not arrogant;

have humour, but without folly.

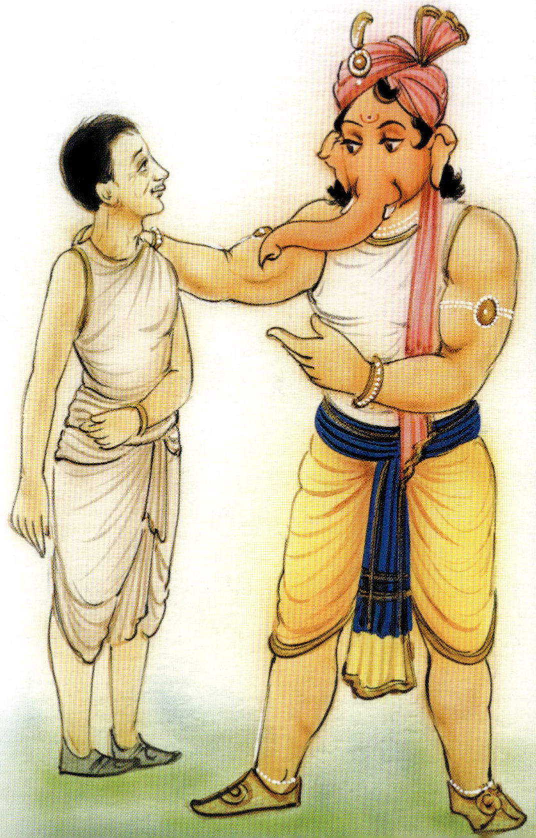

The final test of a leader is
that he leaves behind him
in others the conviction
and will to carry on.

The first responsibility of a leader is to define reality.

The last is to say thank you.

In between, the leader is a servant.

The goal of an effective leader is
to recondition his team
to be solution-focused
rather than problem-focused.

The key to successful leadership,
today,
is influence, not authority.

L-81

The leader has to be
practical and a realist.

Yet, must talk the language
of the visionary and the idealist.

The leader must know,
that he knows,
and must be able to make
it abundantly clear
to those around him
that he knows.

The leader should remember:
the value of time,
the success of perseverance,
the pleasure of working,
the dignity of simplicity,
the worth of character,
the power of kindness,
the influence of example,
the obligation of duty,
the wisdom of economy,
the virtue of patience,
the improvement of talent,
the joy of origin.

The leaders who work most effectively,
it seems to me, never say "I".

And that's not because they have
trained themselves not to say "I".

They don't think "I".

They think "we"; they think "team".

They understand their job
to make the team function.

They accept responsibility
and don't sidestep it,
but in success the team gets
the credit . . .

This is what creates trust
and enables one to
get the task done.

The most important strength of
being a leader is maintaining
the desire to learn.

That means learning about oneself,
about one's peers,
and about the people one serves.

The nice thing about teamwork is that you always have others on your side.

The task of the leader
is to get his people
from where they are
to where they haven't been.

The test of leadership
is not to put
greatness into humanity,
but to elicit it,
for the greatness
is already there.

The ultimate measure
of a leader is
not where he stands in
moments of comfort,
but where he stands
at times of challenge
and controversy.

There are two ways
of spreading light:
to be the candle or
to be the mirror
that reflects it.

To be a leader,
you have to make people
want to follow you, and
nobody wants to follow someone
who doesn't know
where he is going.

L-92

To be able to lead others,
a man must be willing
to go forward alone.

True leaders always practise the three R's:

Respect for self,
Respect for others,
Responsibility for
all their actions.

Values
hold the team together,
provide stability for
the team to grow upon,
measure the team's performance,
give direction and guidance and
attract like-minded people.

L-95

Very few of the great leaders
ever get through their careers
without failing,
sometimes dramatically.

When a gifted team
dedicates itself to unselfish trust
and combines instinct
with boldness and effort,
it is ready to climb.

When a team outgrows
individual performance
and learns team confidence,
excellence becomes a reality.

When we dream alone,
it is only a dream,

but when many dream together
it's the beginning of a new reality.

Whether a man is burdened
by power or enjoys power;

whether he is trapped by responsibility
or made free by it;

whether he is moved by other people
and outer forces or moves them
— this is of the essence
of leadership.